A Gallimaufry

Conversations, Observations and Commentary

Jan Hahn

A Gallimaufry: Conversations, Observations and Commentary
ISBN: Softcover 978-1-960326-11-9
Copyright © 2023 by Jan Hahn

All rights reserved. No part of this book may be reproduced or transmitted in any form or by any means, electronic or mechanical, including photocopying, recording, or by any information storage and retrieval system, without permission in writing from the publisher.

Parson's Porch Books is an imprint of Parson's Porch & Company (PP&C) in Cleveland, Tennessee. PP&C is a self-funded charity which earns money by publishing books of noted authors, representing all genres. Its face and voice is **David Russell Tullock** who you can contact at: dtullock@parsonsporch.com.

Parson's Porch & Company *turns books into bread & milk* by sharing its profits with the poor.

www.parsonsporch.com

A Gallimaufry

Contents

Preface	7
A Poem	9
New Patient Interview	11
The Psychiatrist	13
Marriage	17
A Minister's Creed	19
Minister's Creed part 2	21
No Choice	23
Time	25
When I was Young	27
Trust	29
Requiem of Remorse	31
What do People Want?	33
Psalm 1	35
Psalm 2	37
Psalm 3	39
A Gnat	41
Fortune Teller	43
Heart to Heart	46
Little Jim	47
The Golf Course	49
What am I?	51
Daybreak	53
Modern Life	55
Stand-off	57
To Be Brave or Not to Be-that is the Question	59
Passion	61
Love	63
Veterinarian's Prayer	65
Challenge	67
Life	69
Alone	71
In Praise of Americans	72

Preface

In my first volume of poetry, titled *VOICES*, I introduced my readers to a few of the many patients I have had the privilege of caring for during 40 years of family practice. I let them speak in their own words of the crises afflicting them and their attempts, sometimes successful but often futile, to overcome the challenges they faced.

In this volume I share with you a few more of my patients' stories.

But most of the poems in this volume are my observations and commentary about our world.

Some are dramatic and quite serious; some are playful and even quirky.

It is a potpourri, a salmagundi, a gallimaufry to say the least.

Enjoy.

Jan Hahn

A Poem

At noon, I thought,
How could I express what he so clearly meant?
What choice of words would catch the ear
and voice what he so wanted us to hear?

A poem is like a house.

Foundation first, and then the walls.
And in the time from work to home,
I capped a roof upon the frame.
Then, by foot, wandered for a while,
tinkering quietly in my mind.

And by the end, nailed it tight.

New Patient Interview

I enter---a stranger to you.
And you---a mystery to me.
We have so little time to meet each other. But the playing field is uneven
for I write the rules.
I ask, I interrogate, I probe
the cause of every scar,
the meaning of each tattoo,
the tales of your marriages, and
the fate of every child.

And you must reply,
for silence could reflect deceit or, perhaps,
a skeleton too dangerous to display.

Yet when you question, my answers are cryptic and brief,
I smile kindly, supremely confident that my refusal
to reveal the slightest of myself
is codified, sanctioned, and irrefutable.
The game goes on until you "quit the field" or
lay stretched upon my table of inquiry
naked, bereft of all defenses and with no place to hide.
Your secrets now belong to me.

The Psychiatrist

I glimpse-if only for a moment- men's natures unadorned.
Hear voices discordant, harsh, and shrill.

I enter with impunity, lands few dare ere to tread and confront with
practiced insouciance dragons fierce and cruel.
I wage wars on my patients' behalf,

Lay siege to castles deep within their minds
and bring to the light of day imprisoned souls locked far away.

Voices

Marriage

A Minister's Creed

Minister's Creed part 2

No Choice

Time

When I Was Young

Trust

Requiem of Remorse

What Do People Want?

MARRIAGE

Introduction

Doctor: "Mrs. Washburn, What is the secret to your extraordinarily long and vibrant marriage?"

Commentary

A wag once remarked that when God created the institution of marriage, it showed unequivocally his wicked sense of humor.
To the contrary, I believe He gave us a taste of Heaven.

Poem

72 years!
And they said it would not last.
We sure showed those "doubtin' Thomases"
We have experienced many joys together.
But Oh, we have had our heartaches.
Heartaches can break a marriage.
They can also make it stronger.
You just got to decide.
He hears everything I say to him.
He just doesn't always listen.
Sometimes, he is a slow learner,
I am a very patient teacher.
The secret to our success?
5 C's: communication, cooperation,
consideration, caring, and compassion.
("And you, sir.")
A lot of "yes Dear"

A Minister's Creed

Introduction

Doctor: "Reverend Sires, I have a question for you. From what wellspring do you draw your inexhaustible supply of hope?"

Commentary

What is religion? To the atheist, it is a sanctioned and codified collection of psychotic delusions. To the theologian, it is what keeps him sane in an insane world.

Poem

I do not believe in miracles.
But I believe that God inspires men to move mountains.
The Heavens, the Heavens belong to the Lord and His hosts.
To us, He has given the world that we may make it like the Heavens.

I believe that every day, God intends to teach me a lesson...
Therefore, I listen carefully to whoever crosses my path
for he just might be His messenger.

Minister's Creed part 2

Introduction

Doctor: "Reverend Sires, I have been thinking about what you told me at our last visit. I am intrigued by your faith. Tell me more."

Commentary

As countless philosophers and theologians have remarked, love is the strongest force in the universe. It cannot be denied its day, regardless of how vigorously its opponents contend.

Poem

Years from now, when historians reflect upon the character of our nation,
they will not be impressed
by the might of our armies or
the heights to which our tallest buildings soared or
even the opulence of our houses of worship.

Rather, they will duly note, so that none forget, how we cared for
the disadvantaged,
the displaced,
the disabled,
the diseased,
and the demented.

We are our brothers' keepers.

One day, each of us will stand alone before the Lord.
We will plead that our acts of merit be weighed heavy in the scales of justice while our acts of omission and commission be ignored.

The Lord will reply,
"My children -the homeless, the widow, the orphan, the frightened, and the weak- in despair, cried out and you turned your head and did not see.
Now, what is it today that you ask of Me?"

No Choice

Introduction

Doctor: "Mr. Andrews, I am aware that life has recently taken a nasty turn."

Commentary

There are, unfortunately, many men who believe they have been and are being perpetually victimized, by others and by society in general. Hence, in their eyes, their acts of violence are justifiable. Nothing relieves their psychic pain more than inflicting physical pain on others. The cries of their victims are music to their ears.

Poem

Her mistake was to walk.
I have been given nothing my entire life.
My father left when I was two to chase another woman.
Mom worked three jobs to keep us safe and alive.
I was raised by my brother who could have cared less.
How poor were we?

Catsup is a vegetable.

And if you close your eyes and pinch your nose, you cannot taste the mold.

In the winter, we let the neighbor's dogs in,
not out of the goodness of our hearts
but so we would not freeze.
I went to school not to learn but to eat.
I cared little for books.

The teachers passed me on each successive year-
-"out of sight, out of mind."
I would have "graduated" but in my senior year, we had to pass an exam.
I didn't-thus, no diploma. They took that away from me.

Got a job in a body shop until the boss found out I could not read.
They took that away from me.
The Army would have had me were my teeth not so bad.
They took that away from me too,
To survive, I picked up garbage and sometimes ate it.
Then came the "Spic's" who work for nothing.
And then again they took that away from me.
When I first me Wanda, it was as if I had been given a gift.

She was like me-scarred and bitter.

We had our moments of heaven but too often hell
for I am not easy to live with.

She gave as good as she got. See this scar?
But she shouldn't have walked.

Sometimes, doc, a man has to take a stand, or he ceases to be a man.

Can you not understand?
I had to shoot her.
I had no choice.

Time

Introduction

Doctor: " Ms. Wilson, Your face tells me that you are worried. What is your concern?"

Commentary

As we age, both our physical and cognitive capacities decline. I think people have an easier time
accepting the loss of physical strength than the loss of cognitive skills. for the latter is what gives them their sense of humanity and uniqueness.

Poem

There was a time when time seemed infinite
and pleasures to be enjoyed too many to count

Careless, I squandered the gifts of youth and health.
Now, I cannot remember my memories
and time has neither meaning nor measure.

When I was Young

Introduction

Doctor: "Mr Ayres, How can I help you today?"

Commentary

As we age, there is the inevitable loss of physical strength. Most of us, with quiet resignation and sometimes, a sense of humor, accept our rapidly growing list of limitations. A few of us refuse to accept the crush of reality and to the end, in the words of Dylan Thomas, "Rage, rage against the dying of the light".

Poem

When I was young, I could move mountains.
I ran up hills and never lost my breath.
Sleep was for the weak.
Two hours-batteries recharged- I rushed into the fray again.
Sex, food, drugs-- all fed my voracious appetite.
Now I am old.
My aching knees hobble each step I take.
And I shuffle slowly lest I fall and no one is around to help me up.
I'm a fat and cannot even see what makes me a man
were it to ever rise again.
Sleep beckons me upon the hour and readily
I succumb to its alluring voice.
Yet, never do I seem to get enough.
When I was young, I could not imagine a life where I could not subdue
Any who challenged me.
When I was young, the sun bowed to my demands.
When I was young, the moon did my bidding.
When I was young, the tides answered to me.
But now I am old,
very old, very, very old.
And unless, Doc, you are a wizard,
there is not a damn thing you can do about it.

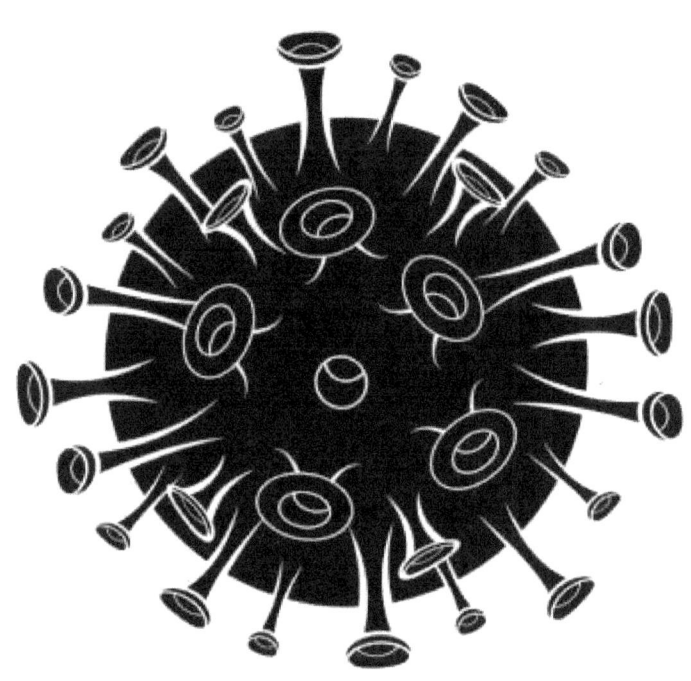

Trust

Introduction

Doctor: "Richard, so are you going to get the Covid vaccination today?"

Commentary

This disconnect between this man's absolute refusal to accept vaccination (the only way to prevent or at least mitigate the severity of infection) and his child-like belief that as long as his physician is around to care for him, he will be safe is infuriating. This attitude often leads doctors to doubt their commitment to the profession and their patients.

Poem

I ain't getting it!
It's a hoax!
The vaccines don't work.
It's a Chinese weapon.

I don't believe a thing you say!

It messes with my DNA.
It makes me magnetic.
I can now be tracked by the NSA.
It causes infertility.

You need more reasons?

I am young and strong and healthy.
I believe in Jesus.
I don't trust the government.

So don't waste your breath, Doc!

I do have one question though.
If I do get sick, will you care for me?
You will-thanks-- I knew I can trust you.

Requiem of Remorse

Introduction

Doctor: "John, I can sense your sadness as soon as I walked in. What is the problem?"

Commentary

Depression is the black hole of emotional disorders. It is so impenetrable that light can neither enter nor leave the soul. It weighs upon the shoulders of the strongest man until his knees buckle and his back breaks. It turns bitter the sweetest of joys, extinguishing, with implacable force, all sense of hope.

Poem

I am entangled by a world of things,
imprisoned by creatures of my own designs,
unhappy slave to a god called Mammon.
Like a ship without a pilot's compass,
I drift aimlessly,
while the years pass quickly, devoid of meaning.
Blind to my true nature and ignorant of my purpose,
I cannot hear God inviting me to the divine dance called Life.
Estranged from myself, I find no pleasure
in the company of others.
And my time on earth-not a gift but a sentence.

What do People Want?

Introduction

Doctor: "Robert, I understand you ran for the House of Representatives this past year. Let me here your stump speech."

Commentary

My step-mother-in-law, the late Senator Annabelle Clement Obrien, the First Lady of Tennessee Politics, once said to me, "Jan, Politics is a beautiful word. I have seen politicians build schools, construct hospitals, and lay down roads. There is no greater honor for a citizen than to be chosen by one's fellow citizens to write the laws that govern their relationships to one another. Yes, politics is a beautiful word."

--The author of this book ran unsuccessfully for the House in November 2022.

What Do People Want?

- That the land they walk upon is safe
- That the air they breathe is clean
- That the water they drink is unpolluted
- That they work at a job
    - that is safe
    - that makes them proud of their participation in the workforce
    - that at the end of the day gives them a living wage

What Do People Want?

They want food that is plentiful and nourishing.
They want to know that if they are felled by injury or illness, there will be arms to raise them upright and hands to bind their wounds.

What Do People Want?

They want to know that when their children go out to play, they will return unharmed.
They want to know that if in the shrouds of darkness, the wrath of Nature were to descend and in its fury destroy all in its path, relief will arrive at the rising of the sun and stay for as long as it is needed.

What Do People Want?

They want their children educated in schools that
- acknowledge, recognize and honor their differences
- help them identify their interests, develop their talents and applaud their accomplishments
- teach them to be critical thinkers capable of independently evaluating competing theories and deciding which lies closer to the truth
- makes them enthusiastic and conscientious participants in a civil democratic society

They want to believe that when they enter their respective houses of worship, they need not fear the taunts of strangers or a hail of bullets or the blast of a bomb.

>These are not Republican needs.
>These are not Democratic goals.
>These are not Independents' aspirations.

>These are all of our most fervent desires.

We are facing unprecedented challenges. The tasks confronting us are many and severe. The time allotted grows shorter by the day. I believe with all my heart and with all my soul
that if we are

>United by common goals
>Respectful of our differences.
>Committed to success.

>We can begin our work today, now.

Psalm 1

Joyful is the one who shuns the path of evil men,
and spurns the words of the wicked,
and turns his back upon the spiteful and the cruel.

Joyful is the one who heeds the commandments of the Almighty
and, daily ponders their meaning.

He shall blossom like a flower,
Warmed by the mid-day sun and bathed by gentle rains.
All his endeavors will be crowned with success.

But the evil man - he shall be tossed like dust in a windstorm.
He shall be ignored, forgotten, and doomed.
His fate will lead him to the abyss.

Psalm 2

Consumed by anger, idol worshippers spew forth obscenities.
Their generals prepare for war while their rulers
Conspire against the Lord and His people, saying
"Let us sever our bonds with them and pitch them to the dirt."

But the Lord laughs, contemptuous of their boasts.
His wrath knows no bounds.

The Lord replies,
"My son rules. To him I gift all. Those who doubt me
and those who challenge me, he shall crush like an eggshell and
shatter like glass.
Pay heed to My words lest you perish
at the hands of My son."

Psalm 3

Sing to the Almighty

Bow deep with a heart filled with love.
Serenade Him with songs of praise
For the Lord is our Maker
We are His children, His lambs.
Open the doors of His palace
Enter His abode with joy
Announce to all His majesty for
His love is everlasting and
Your children will be forever rewarded

A Gnat

One fine summer day, a gnat upon my cheek did lay.
Little did he know how fateful was his choice for a moment's pause.
I raised my hand to crush his tiny frame and
There he stood, unaware of how his life was never going to be the same.
Who am I to render judgment so severe?
What crime did he commit that only death could pay?
In this vast cosmos we call the universe,
Is one gnat more important than another?
And so I gently brushed him off.

Fortune Teller

I'll tell the truth in such a way, a lie could not be different.

I'll give you hope, then cast your fate.

I'll take the measure of your soul
And ply the strings upon your heart,
Knowing neither melody nor score.

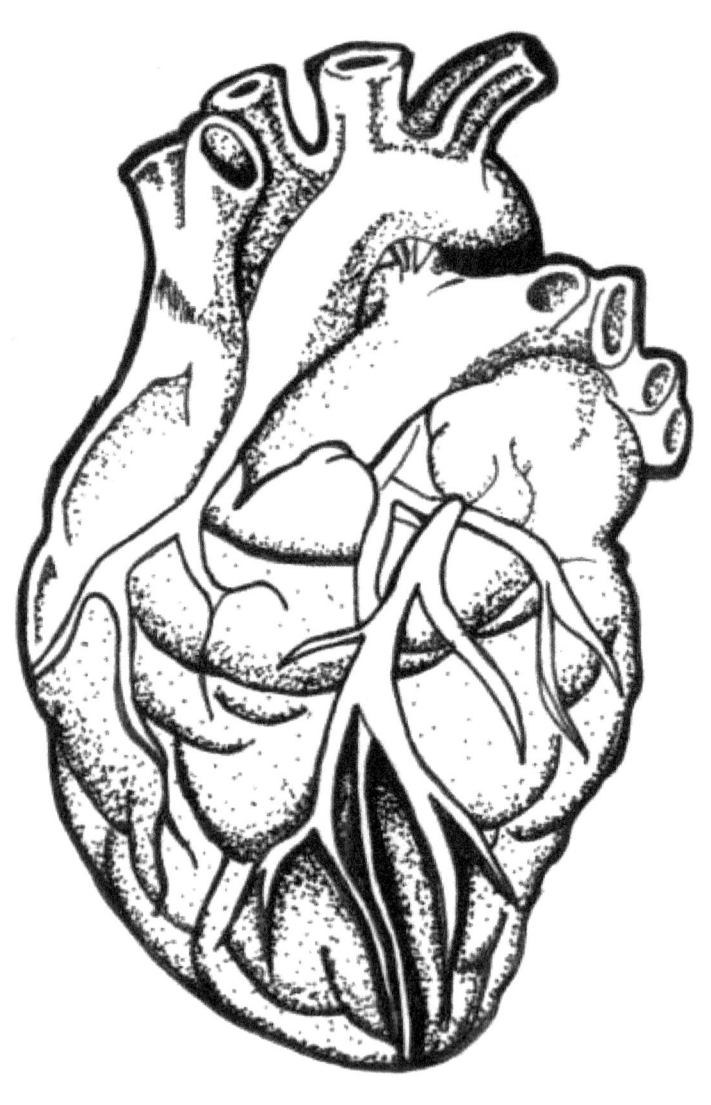

Heart to Heart

A tiny little RBC decided to take a trip around the vascular tree.
"Where should I begin?" he said to a friend.
"Does it really matter, since where you start, you'll always end?"
"Left ventricle is where I'll start!"
And lo and behold, the aortic valve did part.
Down the aorta, he rapidly strode,
Until he met an arteriole where the blood flow slowed.
Next he got lost in a capillary.
"Oh, I wish I had a dromedary!
But the cells need their food and since I am a conscientious dude,
I will unload my supply and then say good-bye."
Into a venule, a tiny vein, he went,
Thoroughly tired, thoroughly spent.
The going was hard, the going was tough,
For he found himself burdened with all sorts of STUFF.
Carbon dioxide and waste galore,
None of which he had bargained for.
Into a vein, he finally moved
And now his spirits markedly improved.
For at its end, the right atrium sat
Which was precisely where he was headed at.
Right atrium to the right ventricle through the tricuspid
Not the mitral, that is a bicuspid.
Into the lung he quickly hastened,
As if behind him a pack of wolves was chasin'.
There he unloaded his STUFF with a nod,
And clasped an 02 to his tiny little bod.
Do I see what I believe?
Do I believe what I see?
Is that not the left atrium staring at me?
I almost home!" he said with a shout.
"No need to worry, no need to pout.
That was a trip, an adventure for sure,
But after some rest, I'm ready for another tour."

Little Jim

An adventurous soul named Little Jim,
Climbed up a tree to test a limb.
The journey up was long, hard, and slow,
The return-not so!

The Golf Course

A cemetery stillness pervades this patch of earth.
Mute testimony of man's perverted sense of play.
Unnatural greenness,

Geometric designs-framed by reason and suspended in time.

A vision of Heaven; a taste of Hell.

What am I?

A plume of smoke-a whistle clear and shrill.
A rumble deep within-a shaking to and fro.
I soothe the coughing child and
Cap the evening's meal.

Daybreak

The river's song of sea and sun,
Transformed to misty melody,
A ship piled high with bags of grain,
Floats quietly, tethered to the dock.
Chased by the icy breath of wind, the sun-singed clouds descend
And silently rush upon the land
'till all substantial seems a dream

And cupolas, like airy charms, float silently upon a sea of clouds.
Then, sans notice, life erupts.
Thoroughfares throng with crowds,
The din so loud no man can talk,
And birds, in joyous exaltation, serenade the world.
Alone, a tired woman walks,
Her face as pale as moonbeams' light,
Her hair, unwashed and loosely bound,
With lips of passion and hateful soul, stares dully at the ground.

Modern Life

The harried sense of hurried life,
The ceaseless din of endless strife,
The pressured urge to fill our store,
Until our arms can hold no more.
There's no time for a neighbor's sorrow,
Our games can't wait until tomorrow.
We reside in homes fit for queens,
Yet homeless walk our streets unseen.
A silly slight-we scream, "My soul is gored!"
But grievous wrong towards a friend is ignored.
The world revolves 'round "I",
And thus, our God did die.

Stand-off

God!
I did not curse thee when upon my shoulders you poured sorrow and grief,
covered me with ash and left me in despair.
Now the sun shines bright and people sing aloud my name.
But do not think I will praise thee for my good fortune.
That misfortune which I endured, I did not deserve.
I merited a kinder fate.
Against thee, I cannot argue.
Your judgment- always sure; your sentence -always just.
I stand alone and to thy face, contend.
"What came, came.
What is, is.
What will be, will be.
And now I take my leave!

To Be Brave or Not to Be-
that is the Question

One might as well rail against the rising of the tides or
Protest the waning of the moon or
Defy the grip of gravity or
Race the light of the setting sun.
Why argue against that for which there is no answer or
Try to change that which is immutable?
Better to bend with the wind
Then break in obstinate defiance.

Passion

(Infidelity's Lament)

The crimson blush of passion spreads slowly across thy chest

more enticing in my sight than a string of pearls or diamond brooch upon a golden leaf.
Your voice-angel, saint, and sinner- sends operatic peals
across our bedded stage,
And time stands still yet moves too fast while night
gives way today.
My resolve succumbs to your caress.
Good intentions led astray.

A night of pleasure beyond compare and now
a life of unremittent despair.

Love

Tell me the source of your youthful beauty.
Did you quench your thirst with an elixir that washes away the wages of time?
Did you eat forbidden fruit that erases years of toil?
Share now with me your dreams and your fondest wishes.
And one by one, I shall answer each command
And when the list has reached its end,
We'll start again..

Thus love animates the dormant soul,
drives darkness from the deepest recesses of the mind and
sets afire the heart's desires.

Veterinarian's Prayer

God hath made the mite and mighty.
Calls worm "His own" and tiger "son."
Then sends them here for safe keeping.

Asks only that we love them true.
"Watch carefully My gifts to thee,
For love of them is praise of Me."

Challenge

Confront each crisis with measured gaze and steadfast resolve
And no challenge will be beyond your strength.
For an anxious soul and fearful gaze distort one's sight,
Turning midgets into monsters and butterflies into dragons.

Life

The gentle kindness of the unexpected gift,
Your strong, steady hand when knees begin to buckle,
Your soothing voice when sorrow sears my frightened soul,
Your quiet presence when loneliness seems my fate,
We enter this world alone; we depart the same,
But on the journey that we call Life,
We must each other's hands hold tight.

Alone

Often, I walk alone or so it might seem to a passer-by.

No I-phone, no I-pad
No Nook, no Kindle Nada, nothing
Zero,
Zilch.
"Aren't you bored?"
My youngest asks.
"Ah, quite the contrary"
I reply.
"My thoughts are good companions."

IN PRAISE OF AMERICANS

(During the time of the Covid pandemic.)

I come to praise.

I sing the praises of the EMT's, firemen, and police officers who each morning donned their uniforms, faced the Angel of Death and said, "F...you. I have a job to do"

I sing the praises of the construction workers, road crews, and truck drivers who each morning put on their boots, faced the Angel of Death and said, "Move aside, bitch. I have homes to build, roads to repair and food to deliver."

I sing the praises of the store managers who set aside specific hours for the elderly and vulnerable that they might shop in safety.

I sing the praises of teachers who knew that their work secures this country's future and devised new ways to teach their students, confused and terrified by a world turned upside down.

I sing the praises of doctors, nurses and all those engaged in the care of others who every day faced the fury of the beast and though they witnessed the deaths of many of their comrades, never fled the field of combat.

I sing the praises of the many thousands sequestered in their homes who made masks and shields so those who fought were protected.

I sing the praises of the ministers and rabbis, the priests and imams who, in the midst of the howling winds of the tempest never let their voices grow dim and in doing so, enabled us to keep our faith.

I sing the praises of all Americans who having been dealt a rotten hand, played on, never folded, and in the end, prevailed.

Let it be noted and never forgotten--- courage resides not in those who are unafraid
but in those, who despite their fears, refuse to retreat.

May God bless America and keep her safe. And let us now say "Amen."

www.ingramcontent.com/pod-product-compliance
Lightning Source LLC
Chambersburg PA
CBHW050446010526
44118CB00013B/1700